An Exhibition

on the Occasion of

1942 - 1992

the Fiftieth Anniversary

of Houghton Library

CENTURIES

Collectors and Friends

OF BOOKS &

Scholars and Librarians

MANUSCRIPTS

Build the Harvard College Library

THE HARVARD COLLEGE LIBRARY · CAMBRIDGE

DISTRIBUTED BY
THE HARVARD UNIVERSITY PRESS

COPYRIGHT 1992
BY THE PRESIDENT AND FELLOWS OF HARVARD COLLEGE.
LIBRARY OF CONGRESS CATALOG CARD NUMBER: 92-70105

With our eye on the next fifty years,
we dedicate this exhibition to those special friends
of learning and teaching who devote themselves to books:
may they—collectors, benefactors, scholars,
librarians, and booksellers—continue
to build up the collections generously,
wisely, and courageously.

PREFACE

T HE CATALOGUE YOU HOLD IN YOUR HANDS—and the innovative exhibition that it accompanies and records—together mark the fiftieth anniversary of the opening of the Houghton Library, the rare book and manuscript library of Harvard College. Catalogue and exhibition alike have been carefully designed to open your eyes to the variety and breadth of the Library's collections.

The richness of these collections has frequently been extolled and described, often quite memorably. Twenty-five years ago, during Houghton's first great anniversary celebration, the Library published a sumptuous record of its treasures with the subtitle "A Selection of Books and Manuscripts in Harvard Collections." That handsome indigo volume, compiled by William H. Bond and designed by Roderick Stinehour, has in a sense begun to become what it described, for it is hard to find, sometimes expensive to purchase, and successfully imitative—in its printing and design—of the great books and manuscripts it celebrates.

The present catalogue is also a selection of books and manuscripts in Harvard collections, but its emphasis falls both on well-known works that have historically formed the center of its collections *and* on a sometimes radically diverse group of materials—diverse in language and cultural context, diverse in origin and use, diverse in format and physical structure. The selections range in date from a ninth-century vellum fragment of Saint Isidore of Seville to a Samizdat publication by Vaclav Havel of 1975. Included are works by Alberti, Delacroix, and Julia Cameron; first editions of Copernicus and Newton; manuscripts of Father Rasle and Trotsky; literary works of Jacopo Sannazaro, Thomas Wolfe, and John Updike; music manuscripts by Beethoven, Schubert, and Schönberg; a dance manual by Gregorio Lambranzi, and a stage prop for the Mabou Mines production of Samuel Beckett's *The Lost Ones.* Rarely before, I imagine, have Hugo von Hofmannsthal and Frank Lloyd Wright been juxtaposed with *The Yellow Kid*, progenitor of the pulp comics.

Such diversity and breadth are the fruits of incessant collecting on behalf of the Harvard College Library during the past two and a quarter centuries. Following the fire of 1764 that virtually destroyed the original library at Harvard, the University's librarians and faculty members—with the devoted support of collectors and friends—built often unparalleled collections in an astonishing range of scholarly disciplines. The present catalogue is therefore dedicated to the many individuals who have made both Houghton and the Harvard College Library international centers for teaching and learning.

This catalogue and exhibition are part of a year-long celebration of the Library's past and—just as significantly—an examination of the long-range future of institutions such as ours. I therefore take pleasure in thanking the entire staff of the Houghton Library for its generous support of this enterprise, and extend my warmest appreciation to Anne Anninger (Philip Hofer Curator of Printing and Graphic Arts) and Roger Stoddard (Curator of Rare Books) for producing such a lively and imaginative response to what is an important (but surely should not be a grave or tedious) occasion. We are delighted that Roderick Stinehour so readily agreed to design our fiftieth (as well as our twenty-fifth and forticth) publications and we thank those close friends of the Library whose loyalty and generosity have enabled us to celebrate our anniversary in such a fitting way both here in Cambridge and, later this Spring, at the Grolier Club in New York City.

RICHARD WENDORF
Librarian

INTRODUCTION

THE CONSTRUCTION of the Houghton Library and its opening on February 28, 1942, signaled an important turning point at Harvard. For the first time rare books and manuscripts would be featured instead of merely guarded. Freed from the locked, grill-front cases of Gore Hall and the dusty permanent exhibitions of the Treasure Room, Harvard's collections would be spread out in the lobby, exhibition room, and second-floor cases of the new library. Over a hundred separate collections came to be displayed there. Services for readers were vastly improved, with an expanded reference collection close at hand, the beginning of a modern rare books catalog with all its separate files, and several years later the establishment of a Manuscript Department with its new cataloging principles.

Hand in hand the Reading Room and Exhibition Room worked together, changing the collections and access to them while responding to changes in readership. The graceful new building in the library center of the Yard made a statement: come inside, and please bring along either your research notes or your collection of rare books and manuscripts! No one could have predicted the success that Houghton's founding librarian William Jackson and his comrade Philip Hofer would have in collecting great European books and great American literary manuscripts. In less than ten years the library expanded into a whole floor of the Lamont Library; later it claimed significant space in Pusey.

Meanwhile the senior scholars and editors who first entered the doors of Houghton were joined by graduate students and undergraduates. Today the Harvard readership is equally divided among them. Original research was always the theme of Houghton Library; now it is a hallmark of Harvard undergraduate education. Seminars held at Houghton by the faculty, courses taught by Houghton staff, and the complexion of the reference collection reflect the change in readership. It is official now: scholars of the future can begin to work independently as undergraduates.

Not even the collections remain the same, and that is the theme of this exhibition. The power of the Houghton Library, like the power of the Harvard Library, regenerates when the acquisitions of the past month or year or decade juxtapose with the historical collections. It is a cumulative renovation. Without the collections of the past any recent increment would be senseless, peripheral, confusing; the use of such isolated fragments would be hazardous and risky for any scholar or student. Without new acquisitions the collections of the past would be unsound, undependable, misleading; the use of such flawed resources would be delusive. The vitality of scholarship is *its* cumulative renovation.

The time is always right for librarians to make exhibitions. All at once they can thank their benefactors, applaud their predecessors, and inform their readers. Special occasions call for a special look at the whole library. And thus, the exhibits selected this time represent a manifold range of books and manuscripts acquired since 1764, the year when fire destroyed the College Library and important new gifts of books and manuscripts were solicited and received. Each of the exhibits is intended for a particular spot in a radically re-configured set of spaces in the Houghton Exhibition Room. Bart Uchida, a brilliant designer of exhibitions, has worked with the librarians to create a new effect. Never before have so many items been shown there, never before have so many modes of display been attempted there, never before has there been such a concerted plan for maximizing the exhibits and minimizing the room.

And the annotations, this time, are bifurcated: there is a note on the historical value of each exhibit and one on the human story of its acquisition by Harvard. You can see how families have turned to the Harvard Library as a safe place to preserve a treasured book or manuscript, how hobbies have been transformed into research collections, how much the materials of scholarly inquiry depend on collaborations that librarians and faculty encourage with well-wishers, alumni, collectors, and bookdealers. The needs of the faculty, the needs of the students have driven Harvard librarians over the years to predict the future by extending the collections into undeveloped and neglected fields so that the library would be prepared to support the work of new generations of scholars.

Looking in new ways at old books and manuscripts is a basic responsibility of the library as a teacher of teachers and a goad of scholars. There are plenty of book warehouses, but there are few libraries that fulfill their responsibilities through the agency of curators and librarians who inhabit their collections, guiding readers and learning from them, testing collections against bibliographies and bookdealers' catalogues and private collections, handling and comparing and exhibiting and cataloging. Original research depends on original collections, acquired item by item over the years and guided by an active intelligence: Centuries of Books and Manuscripts.

ANNE ANNINGER

ROGER STODDARD

CATALOGUE

1 Saint Isidore of Seville, d. 636. Etymologiae; fragment. MS. on vellum. St. Emmeram, Germany, ca. 800. ◆ Irish majuscule script, with capitals touched in red or yellow or surrounded by red dots. Acquired as a teaching example of a bookhand not previously represented in the Library. From the collections of G. Libri and Sir Thomas Phillipps.

Purchased (1976) with funds given by Stanley J. Kahrl, H 1953, PhD 1962, a medievalist who supported the collecting of early manuscripts and theatre history at Harvard. His bequest established fellowships for visiting scholars in theatre history and literary manuscripts.

4

2 Horace. *Opera Omnia.* Germany, 11th century. MS. on vellum, first eight leaves supplied in a fifteenth-century hand. ◆ Scholia attributed to Pomponius Porphyrion. From the collections of the Marquess of Blandford, John Mitford, and Sir Thomas Phillipps.

Purchased (1950) with funds given by Stephen W. Phillips, H 1895, antiquary of Salem.

3 Pope Gregory I, ca. 540–604. Moralia in Job, books 23–29. MS. on vellum. Germany, 12th century. ◆ From the Bibliotheca Conoviana, Dublin; James Elwin Millard; and Henry White collections.

Given (1946) by Dr. William Inglis Morse, Honorary Curator of Canadiana, whose benefactions enriched the collections with early Canadian manuscripts.

4 Book of Hours, usage of Rome, in Latin and French. France, Burgundy, ca. 1485. ◆ MS. on vellum with twenty-four miniatures in tempera and gold by the Master of the Burgundian Prelates.

Bequeathed (1874) by the Honorable Charles Sumner, H 1830, senator from Massachusetts from 1851 to 1874. The twenty-five manuscripts in Sumner's bequest represented the largest acquisition of early manuscripts to be received by the College since its foundation: Sumner doubled the collection. His personal papers, another part of his bequest, are a major historical source for our knowledge of Abolitionism.

5 Gutenberg Bible. [Mainz, ca. 1454–55]. 2 vols. ◆ The Gutenberg Bible or, as it is also known, the 42-line Bible, was printed at Mainz before 24 August 1456. The text is the Paris recension of St. Jerome's Latin Vulgate version. The printing is ascribed to Gutenberg, who is credited with the invention of printing with moveable type. The Harvard copy is one of twenty surviving complete copies. A spectroscopic analysis of its ink, page by page, has yielded new discoveries about the production of the first printed Bible. (*Publications of the Bibliographical Society of America* 81 (1987): 403–32.)

Presented (1944) by Mr. George Widener and Mrs. Eleanor Widener Dixon. The Bible was originally purchased in 1912 by P.A.B. Widener, who intended to present it to his grandson, Harry Elkins Widener, H 1907. An avid collector, the young Widener perished in the Titanic catastrophe before he could be given the Bible. In 1915 a new library was dedicated in his memory. His collection of English literature is displayed in the Harry Elkins Widener Memorial Room.

6 Marcus Valerius Martialis. *Epigrammata.* [Venice, 1469–72]. ◆ Editio princeps, printed in Roman types by Vindelinus de Spira and edited by Georgius
Merula. "Firsts" of the Greek and Roman classics, evocative Renaissance documents of
both scholarship and typography, have attracted Harvard's alumni, faculty, and librarians, so that a very full collection of them has been assembled.

Given (1945) by Boies Penrose II, H 1925, student of early English travellers
abroad and collector of their books.

7 Apocalypsis Sancti Johannis. [German? ca. 1462?] ◆ Blockbook, so called be-
cause both pictures and text are cut and printed from the same woodblock; no
printing types are used. Printed in brown, on one side of the leaf. In this copy the hand
coloring is contemporary with the printing. This is the Servais-d'Ourches-Renouard-
Holford copy, one of four copies in the United States.

Purchased (1947) with funds provided by Philip Hofer, H 1921, LHD 1967, one of
the greatest of all the benefactors of the Harvard Library. He gathered a unique collection of materials in the graphic arts and founded in 1938 the Department of Printing
and Graphic Arts in the Harvard College Library.

7

דשאין לתקן תקנות בעניין בעצמן גל אופמני ינא אח שאפ
שירצו ילכגוס לבל העוכר על תקנותם ב
בלא בשאין אדם גדול וחכם ב
בעיר לתקן עניינם
אבל אם
יש
חכם ומב
ומנהג אפילו כל ב
בני העיר אין רשאין לתקן כל
בלום זולתו אם תקנו והתנו דבר מבלתי ידיעתו
איגו בלום
הלב

המוכר לחבירו דבר במרה
או במשקל או במניין נס
וטעה אפילו בכל שהוא ח
חוזר לעולם שלא אמרו מחילה בטעות משחות אל
אלא כשטעו בשומא אבל טעו באחד מאלו חוזר לע
לעולם והמקח קיים ומחזירין הטעות בין אם ש
טעה הליסח ונתן לו יתרון בין אם טעה
החובר וסבל פחות ובן אם ס
טעו בעניין המעות
שנמצא ח
חסרון
או
יתרון על חנעיין שפסקו חוזרין לעולם לתבוע ח
היתרון
או החיסרון ואפיל
אם לא תבעו היתרון אם הוא
בפרי שהדעת טועה בגון לפי הגונהב סר
שרגילין למנות או שלשה שלשה או ארבע ארבע וגו
ומצא חשבון של בב או גג או דד או יותר חי
חייב להחזיר דאיבא למימר
רטעה בחשבון ובן
אם מצא
עשר
פעמים בב או גג או יותר איבא למימ טעה בעשיריות
אבל אם אין החשבון יוצא לפי חנעיין ש
שרגילין למנות בו אין צריך
להחזיר דאיבא לט
למימר נ
מתנה
ביון
ליתן לו או גזלו ו
ומתבייש להודיעו וכיון לחב
לחבליעו בחשבון דחח לבל חנוסך בל מע
מעות מחבירו בין בתורת הלואה בין בתור פיך
פרעון ואפילו לא היה לו שום עסק ע
עמו טעילם איבא למימר דאי
דאיצ אחרינא פיגזל
צולי ובל
לחאי
בי אהא פלוגי גב אבלע ליה בחשביין ובתב הרם
בס אפילו צוד מירו שלא נשאר בידו כלום הוי סב
סגיין סעות וחונד ובתב הראבד פעמים שהמסה

בסל וחוזר בו על זמן שלא השלים לו ביצד היה ת
תומפ שם מלא אגוזים ואל חילר סף נח
בגיר ויש בו סאה של אגוזים
נהלך דמרדו ולא ח
היה בו ס
סאה
הרי זה חוזר את על
פי שזה רוצה להשלים לו חס
חסאה אבל אם היה לפניו סף של אגוזי
דזה ידע שאין בו שיעור מרח וזה אומר הגה לך ס
סאה של אגוזים בריג ונטלו ומרדו ולא
מצא בו מרח הרי זה סגה ויש
וישלים שהרי זה ת
היה מכיר
שלא
היה בו סאה ועל דעת שישלים לו נטלו

מכר חפץ לחבירו ונגמ ע
בו מום שלא י
ירע בו חלום
מחזירו אפילו אחר כמה ימים שזהו מסח טעות ו
ודוא שלא נשתמש במטח אחר שירע הטום אבל ב
בשתמש במסח אחר שירע הטום הרי זה מחלו ואיא
יבול להחזיר בו אין נוחשבין פחת הטום
אפילו מבר לו חפץ שוה מאה
ריגרין ונמצא בו ע
מום הע
המפחיתו באיסר מ
מחזיר לו הבלי ואיגו יבול ל
לומר אחזיר לך בשיעור פחת הטום שיא
שיאמר הלוסח בחפץ שלם אני רוצה ובן אם ירצה
הלוסח לסחת פחת חמום חרשות ביד ה
המוכר לומר או סח אותו כמו
שהוא או תסח מע
מעותיר
וחחזיר לי מכ חי ש
שאלה לאא הרזל ראובן ושמ
ושמעון היו באשבלייא ויש לראובן בת
בתים בקרטוב וסגיהם מכירין הבתים והסבימו י
יחר
סימבור ראובן לש
לשמעון הבתים בסכום ממון
ועשו סבסות שלא יחזור בהן ולאחר ג ח
חרשים געשה הטבר ובין החסבמה והמבכר באו גוי
גוים
לסרטובה
וחבו בבתים חחם
וסילסלו בחן מסצת מסומות
ועסגי כותלי הבתים מחמת האש שהרל
שהרליסו בבית ועסרו מסע דלהי חבית והחלוגות
ודוצח
שמעון לחוזור בו בי אומר שנגסלסלח סורם גמר ח
חמסח ודוא לא ירע וחוי מסח טעות וראובן אומ
שהסי לסגול חוא ובר מוטס בגגר ערד הבתים שוח

8

8 Jacob ben Asher, ca. 1269–ca. 1340. *Arba ah turim.* Pieve di Sacco, 1475. ❖ A fourteenth-century code of Jewish civil law that embraced and attempted to rationalize all *halakhot* and customs incumbent upon the individual and the community. Its authority is still recognized. The first book to be printed throughout with Hebrew type.

Given by Lucius N. Littauer, н 1878, who in 1930 purchased *en bloc* for his alma mater the Hebrew book collection of Ephraim Deinard.

9 Peter Schwarz, d. 1481. *Contra perfidos Judaeos.* [Esslingen, 1475]. • Hebraist and polemist, Schwarz (Petrus Niger), a Dominican, was educated in Montpellier and in Salamanca, where he learned Hebrew and compiled anti-Jewish polemical material. Upon his return to Germany, he took part in 1474 in a week-long religious disputation with the rabbis of Regensburg. Many of his arguments were developed in the *Contra perfidos Judaeos,* published the following year. The book contains some Hebrew characters, possibly the first use of such type.

Bequeathed (1957) by Lee M. Friedman, H 1893, scholar and book collector, whose early Judaica is the basis of the Harvard collection. His bequest of funds in support of his collection enabled the Library to establish the position of Lee M. Friedman Bibliographer in Judaica in the Harvard College Library.

10 Aesopus moralisatus. Verona, 1479. • One of the finest Italian illustrated books of the fifteenth century, this Latin edition is accompanied for the first time by the Italian translation and moralities of Accio Zucco. Of twenty copies recorded, this is the only one on recycled vellum, a printed palimpsest.

Purchased (1956) with funds provided by Philip Hofer, H 1921, LHD 1967.

10

SONETTO MATERIALE.

LA rana per uolerse asimigliare
  Al boue de persona e de grandezza
  Se puose a uoller farse a sua gualezza
  E feramente se prese a sgonfiare.
El figlio suo li dice deh non fare
  Per che al boue sei niente de parezza
  E sel non cessa quella tua ferezza
  Ben lieuemente potresti crepare.
Corociossi fiermente alhor la rana
  Ede sgonfiarse sforcia sua natura
  Credendo pur compir sua uoglia uana.
Vnde sgonfiata fuor de la mesura
  L interior li cadde in terra piana.
  Si che diffata iace sua figura.
Non uoglia al grande el picol simigliarsi
Pria se consigli e uoglia temperarsi.

SONETTO MORALE

GVardatiue signor farui ranochia
  Ne ue gonfiati per uoglia superba
  Che la negra palude non ue serba
  Cipriano dice ne Crhisto li adochia

11   Leon Battista Alberti, 1404–1472. *De re aedificatoria*. Florence, 1485. ◆ The fruit of Alberti's long reflection on Vitruvius and on classical architecture, the *De re aedificatoria* improved upon the engineering knowledge of antiquity and fully developed an aesthetic theory based upon the neo-platonic principles of well-ordered forms and harmony. It became the bible of Renaissance architecture. This first edition is dedicated to Lorenzo de' Medici and prefaced by Angelo Poliziano.

      Purchased (1957) with funds presented by Ward M. Canaday, H 1907, and Mrs. Canaday, whose gift of Gentile di Giuseppe's collection of Italian books strengthened Harvard's holdings of Renaissance literature and eighteenth-century fine printing.

12   Homer. Opera, graece. Florence [1488–89]. 2 vols. ◆ Editio princeps edited by Demetrius Chalcondylas. In this copy, the borders on the first page of each volume and the illustrated initials at the head of each book have been illuminated in an antique style—probably in the late seventeenth century.

      Bequeathed (1951) by William King Richardson, H 1880, whose collection, one of the most magnificent that has come to the Houghton Library, includes early manuscripts, incunabula, historic bindings, and French illustrated books of the eighteenth century.

13 Desiderius Erasmus, d. 1536. *Adagiorum collectanea.* [Paris, 1500]. ◆ This edition, the first of Erasmus' collection of sentences, maxims, and proverbs drawn from the Ancients, contains 818 adages, many without commentary. As the years went by, Erasmus continued to collect sentences, adding commentaries in the form of small moral treatises that reconcile the wisdom of antiquity with Christian thought. The last edition published during Erasmus' lifetime contained more than four thousand adages. All the important editions are now at Harvard.

Purchased (1952) with funds received from the sale of duplicates.

14 Girolamo Savonarola, 1452–1498. *Piu opere di fragirolamo di Ferrara.* MS. 1498–99. ◆ The earliest known manuscript for some of the brief texts and letters that make up the volume. It bears the ownership signature of Bartolomeo del Vantaggio, a friend who smuggled papers out of prison for Savonarola. A long-lost MS. from the collection of Miss Countryman of New York.

Given (1971) by the Friends of the Harvard College Library.

15 Jacopo Sannazaro, 1458–1530. *Libro Pastorale nominato Arcadio.* Venice, June 1502. ◆ The true first edition. Only seven other copies are recorded of the work that has ensured Sannazaro's reputation. Celebrated in his own time for the Piscatory Eclogues, he invented a new vernacular form with his *Arcadia,* fusing elements from Greek pastoral literature and from the *Ameto* of Boccaccio. Most obviously influenced were Tasso, Sidney, Shakespeare, and Mozart. From the collection of Bishop Thomas Dampier and the sixth Duke of Devonshire.

Purchased (1982) with the Amy Lowell trust fund, today the principal resource for increasing by purchase the rare book and manuscript collections.

16 Sigismondo Fanti, 16th century. *Theorica et practica . . . de modo scribendi fabricandique omnes literarum species.* Venice, 1514. ◆ The first illustrated manual on the art of writing. Fanti's work gives practical advice on selecting implements, on the correct way of holding the pen, and on spacing letters. More importantly, it is the first book to be illustrated with calligraphic models of the alphabet.

Given (1972) by William Bentinck-Smith, H 1937, who presented in 1955 his historical collection of type specimen books to the Department of Printing and Graphic Arts, together with a fund for further acquisitions. He is the author of *Building a great library, the Coolidge years at Harvard* (1976).

Statua seu Scriptoris Forma.

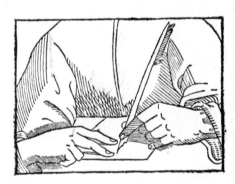

Exemplum Quomodo Calamum aut Pennam cum Ratione tenere Debemus.

17   Lodovico Ariosto, 1474–1533. *Orlando furioso*. Ferrara, 1516.   ✦   The first edition. Only seven other copies are recorded. An original continuation of Boiardo's *Orlando innamorato*, the *Orlando furioso* is a perfect expression of the spiritual values and artistic tendencies of the Cinquecento. Ariosto continued to revise his epic for the rest of his life, the successive versions, most of which are at Harvard, showing the increased influence of Bembo in matters of language and style. Virtually all the important editions are now at Harvard.

Given (1945) by the Friends of the Harvard College Library.

18   Giovanni Giorgio Trissino, 1478–1550. Specimen sheet of printing types. [Vicenza, Tolomeo Gianicolo, 1529]. 28 x 35 cm.   ✦   In his 1524 *Epistola* to Clement VII, the humanist poet Trissino proposed orthographic reforms to the Italian language. These involved the introduction of new letters, the design and casting of which had been entrusted to Ludovico degli Arrighi and Lautizio Perugino, who based their forms on the lovely italic hand employed by the Papal Chancery: Cancellaresca.

Presented (1952) by William Bentinck-Smith, H 1937.

a b c d e f g ch e gh k i l j m n o p q r s t ſ u z v ç. x y th ph h.

A B C D E F G CH C GH K I L I M N O P Q R ω S T Ʒ U Z V Ʒ. X Y TH PH H.

a be ce de e iffe ge che e ghe kia i elle ji emme enne o pe qu erre ω esse te ſe u zes vu çets. icſe fyω the phe haca.

a e i o ω u.   oi au ei eu ei ia ie ie io iω iu oi uo.

ab	ac	ad	af	ag	al	am	an	ap	ar	as	at.
eb	ec	ed	if	ig	el	em	en	ep	er	es	et.
eb	ec	ed	ef	eg	el	em	en	ep	er	es	et.
ib	ic	id	if	ig	il	im	in	ip	ir	is	it.
ob	oc	od	of	og	ol	om	on	op	or	os	ot.
ωb	ωc	ωd	ωf	ωg	ωl	ωm	ωn	ωp	ωr	ωs	ωt.
ub	uc	ud	uf	ug	ul	um	un	up	ur	us	ut.

ba	cha	da	fa	gha	la	ja	ma	na	pa	ra	sa	ta	ſa	za	va	ça.
be	ce	che	de	fe	ge	ghe	le	je	me	ne	pe	re	se	te	ſe	ze	ve	çe.
be	ce	che	de	fe	ge	ghe	le	je	me	ne	pe	re	se	te	ſe	ze	ve	çe.
bi	ci	chi	di	fi	gi	ghi	ki	li	ji	mi	ni	pi	ri	si	ti	ſi	zi	vi	çi.
bo	cho	do	fo	gho	lo	jo	mo	no	po	ro	so	to	ſo	zo	vo	ço.
bω	chω	dω	fω	ghω	lω	jω	mω	nω	pω	rω	sω	tω	ſω	zω	vω	çω.
bu	chu	du	fu	ghu	lu	ju	mu	nu	pu	qua	que	que	qui	ru	su	tu	ſu	zu	vu	çu.

bra chra dre fre ghre pre tri vri bro chro frω grω pru tru sba scu sdiu sfa sgi skia sla sma sno ſpe ſprun ſta ſtrin svo.

O Padre nostro, che ne i cieli stai,
Laudato sia 'l tuo nome, e 'l tuo valore;
Vegna ver noi la pace del tuo Regno.
In terra fatto sia lo tuo volere;
Come si fa ne la celeste corte.
Da hogi a noi la cottidiana manna.
E cosi come il mal, che haven soffirto,
Perdoniamo a ciascun, e tu perdona
Quel, che haven fatto contra i tuoi precetti.
Nun ci tentar con l'antico aversaro;
Ma fa, che siamo liberi dal male.
    Amen.

ΠΑΝΤΟ · · · ΜΕΝΟΝ
T. ·IA·

A ve Maria di molte grazie piena,
Con teco sia l'altissimo Signore.
Tu fra le Donne benedetta sii;
E benedetto il frutto del tuo ventre
Iesu. O Madre de l'eterno Sire,
Porgi i tuoi dolci prieghi inanzi a lui
Per noi, che siamo erranti, e peccatori.
    Amen.

C hi dirà queste in genocki devoto,
Col volto volto verso l'oriente,
E col cappello giu del suo capello,
Spiri, che'l voto suo non sarà voto.

19 Georg Joachim Rhäticus, 1514–1576. *Narratio prima*. Gdansk, 1540. • A young professor of mathematics at Wittenberg, Rhäticus must have heard of the unpublished Copernican theory from Johann Schöner in Nuremberg. Soon after he began visiting the aging Copernicus, Rhäticus was allowed to publish the "first narrative," the earliest printed account of the heliocentric theory of the universe. Extremely rare, this is one of some twenty extant copies.

Presented (1950) by Harrison D. Horblit, H 1933, collector of history of science,

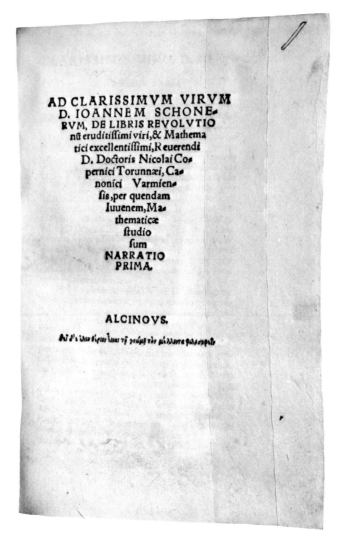

book catalogues, Sir Thomas Phillipps, and early photography. His gift of early printed books and works in astronomy and navigation have ensured the importance of the history of science collections. Some of his gifts are described in an exhibition catalogue entitled *Collector's choice* (1983).

20 Nicolaus Copernicus, 1473–1543. *De revolutionibus orbium coelestium.* Nuremberg, 1543. ◆ As early as 1514, Copernicus circulated privately among friends the *Commentariolus*, a manuscript summary of his heliocentric theory. As the years passed, he developed his arguments with mathematical calculations, hesitating to publish them. It was not until 1540 that the manuscript was taken to Nuremberg and Leipzig and prepared for publication by Andreas Osiander and Johann Schöner. A copy of the *De revolutionibus* is believed to have been brought to Copernicus at Frauenberg on the last day of his life, 24 May 1543.

Presented (1973) by David P. Wheatland, H 1922, collector of books on electricity, early scientific books and instruments. While enriching the collection of manuscripts and printed books in history of science, he founded, arranged, and opened to research the Harvard Collection of Historic Scientific Instruments.

net, in quo terram cum orbe lunari tanquam epicyclo contineri
diximus. Quinto loco Venus nono mense reducitur. Sextum
deniq; locum Mercurius tenet, octuaginta dierum spacio circu
currens. In medio uero omnium resídet Sol. Quis enim in hoc

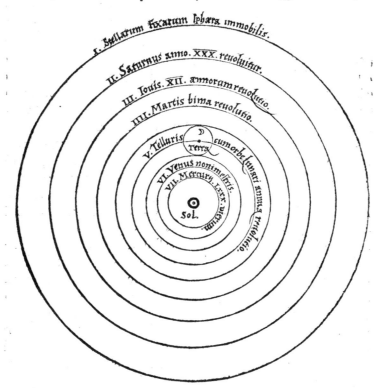

pulcherimo templo lampadem hanc in alio uel meliori loco po
neret, quàm unde totum simul pofsit illuminare? Siquidem non
inepte quidam lucernam mundi, alíj mentem, alíj rectorem uo=
cant. Trimegiftus uisibilem Deum, Sophoclis Electra intuentē
omnia. Ita profecto tanquam in solio re gali Sol residens circum
agentem gubernat Aftrorum familiam. Tellus quoq; minime
fraudatur lunari ministerio, sed ut Aristoteles de animalibus
ait, maximā Luna cū terra cognatioñe habet. Concipit interea à
Sole terra, & impregnatur annuo partu. Inuenimus igitur fub
hac

21

21 Prospero Fontana, ca. 1512–1597. Study for an emblem in Achille Bocchi's *Symbolicarum quaestionum libri quinque*. Bologna, 1555. Pen and brown ink and wash over chalk indications on wove paper. 11.5 x 8.7 cm.
♦ Formerly attributed to Giulio Bonasone (ca. 1498–ca. 1580).

Presented (1982) by David P. Becker, Assistant Curator in the Department of Printing and Graphic Arts from 1975 to 1980, and author of several catalogues for the Department. Among them are *Drawings for book illustration, the Hofer collection* (1980), and, most recently, *The work of Stephen Harvard, a life in letters* (1990).

22 Luis de Camões, 1524?–1580. *Os Lusiadas.* Lisboa, 1572. ◆ Copies of both the "E" and "Ee" editions: the pelican at the top of the title-page faces right in the former and left in the latter. Camões had the chance to retrace Vasco da Gama's pioneer voyagc to India, thc thcmc for this epic poem of the Portuguese empire, and the greatest achievement of Portuguese literature. From the Fernando Palha collection.

Given (1925) in memory of the Count of Santa Eulalia by John B. Stetson Jr., H 1906, Honorary Curator of Portuguese Literature, who established at Harvard a world resource for the study of Portuguese culture with his purchase of the Palha collection of 4600 rare books and manuscripts.

23 Terrestrial globe in gores. Ingolstadt, [ca. 1518]. 20.5 x 31 cm. ◆ Twelve woodcut gores, six of the Old World interlocked with those of the New World, printed on one leaf; the place names are printed from moveable type. This globe, one of the earliest to name America, represents knowledge of the New World ca. 1511–1515, before the new discoveries in the south of Brazil became known.

Northern hemisphere. [Rome?], 1554. 75 cm. in diameter. One of two hemispheric maps engraved by Giulio de' Musi for Michele Tramezzino, publisher and printer of maps. Designed on a "homolographic" or evenly drawn meridian projection as described by Roger Bacon in the thirteenth century. This is one of the few maps from Italy to escape the strong contemporary influence of Gastaldi.

Given by Stephen W. Phillips, H 1895, and by Curt H. Reisinger, H 1912, who presented to Harvard in 1951 the Hauslab-Prince Liechstenstein collection of Renaissance maps, consisting of more than 150 wall and sheet maps, a number of them unique.

24 *Les Trois Grâces.* Color lithograph after Lejeune. Paris and London, 1844. 43 x 34.5 cm. ◆ The three graces, classical personifications of grace and beauty, are transformed here into the three greatest dancers of the Romantic ballet. Wreaths beneath the dancers' feet identify *Taglioni, Fanny Elssler,* and *Miss Ceritto* (actually a representation of Carlotta Grisi).

Bequeathed (1986) by Edwin Binney, H 1946, PhD 1961, Honorary Curator of Ballet in the Harvard Theatre Collection and author of numerous articles and catalogues concerning dance prints. Binney's comprehensive collection of prints of the Romantic ballet is one of the greatest resources of the Harvard Theatre Collection.

25 Gregorio Lambranzi, fl. 1700. *Neue und curieuse theatralische Tantz-Schul.* Nuremberg, 1716. ◆ An eighteenth-century dance manual, in German and Italian, composed of 101 engraved plates by Johann Georg Puschner. Each represents a contemporary dance, complete with tune and brief description. The themes draw upon the lives of peasants, artisans, tradesmen, or soldiers, demonstrating the continued popularity of the Commedia dell' Arte.

Presented (1983) by Philip Hofer, H 1921, LHD 1967, in memory of Helmuth Domizlaff, the great German bookdealer.

26 Johann Christian Bach, 1735–1782. Six Trios for two violins and viola, op. 2. MS. in an unidentified hand. Austria or Italy, second half of the eighteenth century. ◆ The principal source for the work, published from this manuscript in 1937.

Given (1948) by George Benson Weston, H 1897, in memory of his wife Meriel Dimick Weston. Altogether, Weston's gifts include twenty-six early manuscripts of compositions by Bach family members.

27 August von Kotzebue, 1761–1819. *The virgin of the sun. A play in five acts, translated by Anne Plumptre.* London, 1799. ◆ One of several Kotzebue plays adapted for the American stage by William Dunlap (1766–1839), the father of American drama. This is Dunlap's own copy, heavily annotated, most probably for publication as an acting edition.

Bequeathed (1917) by Evert Jansen Wendell, H 1882, whose bequest to Harvard filled a railroad boxcar. Harvard responded by establishing the Portrait Collection in

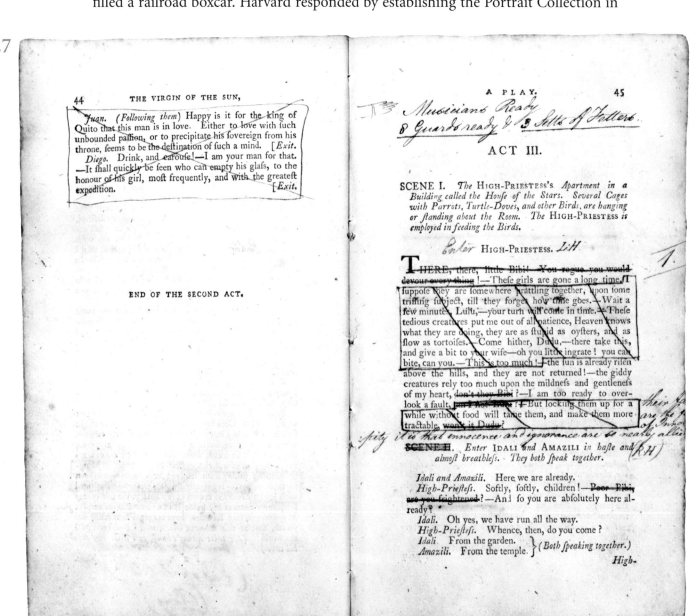

Widener Library and the Autograph File in the Treasure Room. Books and pamphlets filled the American and British book collections in the Widener stacks and hundreds of thousands of ephemeral pieces enriched the Theatre Collection in all its parts.

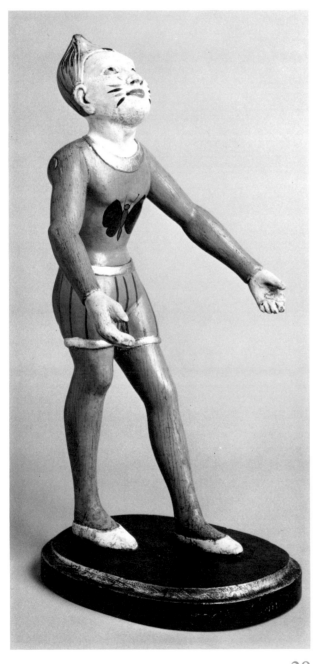

28 Acrobat. Polychrome wooden statuette, [France? mid-19th century]. 38 cm. ⬦ The butterfly emblem on his costume identifies the acrobat as a member of the famous Price circus family. Originally from England, the Price family was active in Denmark from the end of the eighteenth to the early twentieth century.

Bequeathed (1981) by Marian Hannah Winter, author of the *Theatre of marvels* (1948) and *The pre-Romantic ballet* (1974). The Rose Winter and Marian Hannah Winter Memorial Collection illustrates in prints, drawings, and objects what Hannah Winter termed the "theatre of the marvelous," ranging from itinerant musicians on the street corner to the most prestigious international equestrian dancers at the hippodrome.

29   Baseball Songs. Selections from a collection of 153 pieces, commencing with J. R. Blodgett, "The Baseball Polka," Buffalo, 1858.

Given (1961) by Raymond S. Wilkins, H 1912, together with some thirty-three thousand pieces of sheet music, largely from 1890 through 1920, strong in Tin Pan Alley and including over a thousand Rags.

29

30 Dr. John Doran, 1807–1878. *"Their Majesties' servants." Annals of the English stage, from Thomas Betterton to Edmund Kean.* London, 1888. ◆ "Extra-illustrated," Doran's volume was taken apart, inlaid within borders to folio size, and extended to five volumes by the insertion of drawings, engravings, autograph letters, and playbills pertaining to the text. The fashion for extra-illustration was invaluable in preserving ephemeral material that might otherwise have perished. This is one of several such sets in the Harvard Theatre Collection, some of which were bound for Robert Gould Shaw.

Presented (1915) by Robert Gould Shaw, H 1869, who began collecting material on the theatre in his senior year. By 1915, when he had assumed the first curatorship of the Harvard Theatre Collection, Shaw had already assembled one of the two largest theatrical collections in America. The other, formed by his rival Evert Jansen Wendell, came to Harvard by bequest two years later.

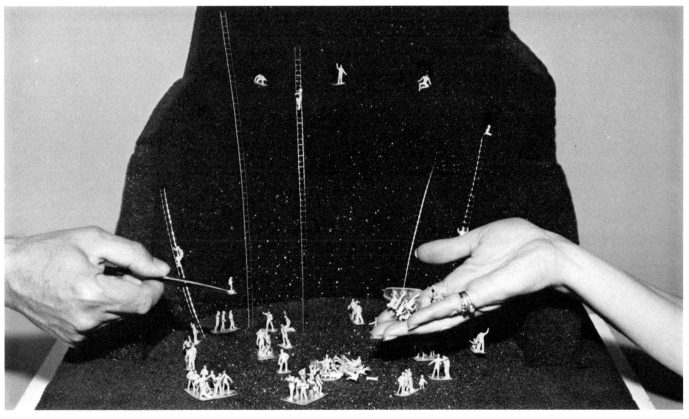

31 Production prop for Samuel Beckett's *The lost ones.* [New York, 1975]. Poly-foam. 53 x 53 x 45 cm. ◆ The Mabou Mines staged Samuel Beckett's short novel *The lost ones* at the Theater for the New City in October 1975. The piece was directed by Lee Breuer. The spectators were seated in a small room entirely lined with dark foam rubber. At the back of the room stood this prop, the "abode where lost bodies roam, each searching for its lost ones." As the performance unfolded, the narrator propped the tiny ladders against the wall and arranged with tweezers the small plastic figurines.

Presented (1977) by Robert D. Graff, H 1941. Sometime television and motion picture producer, Graff formed extensive collections of Samuel Beckett, Sean O'Casey, Antonin Artaud, and others, all of which have come to Harvard.

32 Ludwig van Beethoven, 1770–1827. *An die Hoffnung.* Lied op. 94. Autograph MS., corrected and revised, unsigned. Vienna, 1815. ✦ Also contains a fragment from the last movement of the op. 96 G major violin sonata and the first draft of the canon "Ars longa, vita brevis."

Bequeathed (1925) with other manuscripts and first editions by Amy Lowell, poet and book collector.

33 Ludwig van Beethoven, 1770–1827. *Sonate pour le piano-forte für das Hammer-Klavier des Museum's für Klavier-Musik.* Vienna, [1817]. ✦ Following the death of his brother Caspar Carl in 1815, Beethoven was appointed co-guardian, together with the boy's mother, of his nine-year-old nephew Karl. Difficult years followed for Beethoven, filled with the struggle for possession of his nephew and the burden of caring for a child. Nonetheless, in 1816 he composed two important works, the song cycle *An die ferne Geliebte*, op. 98, and the Piano Sonata no. 28 in A, of which this is the first edition, engraved throughout but for one leaf of advertisement.

Presented (1953) by Mrs. Frederick W. Hilles, daughter of William Inglis Morse. She and her husband are the generous benefactors for whom the Hilles Library is named. Only last year the Susan Morse Hilles Reading Room in the new Fine Arts Library was named for her.

34 Franz Schubert, 1797–1828. *Auf dem Strom.* Lied D 943. Autograph MS., corrected and revised, signed. Vienna? March 1828. ✦ Varies from the published text. Specially composed for the first and only concert of Schubert's own works, held in Vienna on the first anniversary of Beethoven's death, 26 March 1828, *Auf dem Strom* is one of Schubert's last songs (he died on 19 November of the same year). It is the only one of his *Lieder* with a horn obbligato, which supports the voice most impressively. It thus forms a counterpart to *Der Hirt auf dem Felsen*, which has a clarinet obbligato.

Given (1947) in memory of Meriel Dimick Weston by George Benson Weston, H 1897.

35 Robert Schumann, 1810–1856. *Dichterliebe. Liedercyklus aus dem Buche der Lieder von H. Heine.* Leipzig, [1844]. • 1840 has been called the Year of the Song for Schumann who, after an interval of twelve years, returned with a burst of creative energy to the composition of lieder. Following Clara's visit in Leipzig in April, Schumann composed the Eichendorff *Liederkreis* op. 39, immediately followed by a Heine cycle, the *Dichterliebe* op. 48, and four other songs. This is the first edition of the *Dichterliebe*, engraved throughout.

Purchased (1971) with the Susan A. E. Morse fund established by Dr. William Inglis Morse in memory of his wife. As well as Canadiana, Dr. Morse collected and presented to Harvard first editions of music classics.

36 *Como in Italien.* [Germany? ca. 1835]. 17 x 13.5 cm.; unfolds to 37 cm. ✦ This hand-held peep show of Lake Como is typical of mementos sold to European tourists as souvenirs of their visits. From the Renaissance the peep show consisted of a box with an eyehole beyond which unfolded, accordion style, a miniature scene complete with figures, all in perspective. Exciting new structures, cityscapes or idyllic retreats were favorite subjects for peep shows which, today, inform us about the scenes, tastes, and costumes of the period.

Bequeathed (1967) by Susan D. Bliss, collector and donor of festival books and peep shows.

37 Gabriel Fauré, 1845–1924. Quintet no. 2 in C minor for piano and strings op. 115. Autograph MS., signed. [Paris?] March 1921. ✦ Although composed when Fauré was seventy-six, this work is often praised for its freshness and youthful enthusiasm.

Given (1921) by "several donors through the Division of Music," i.e. Mr. and Mrs. Edward Burlingame Hill, and others. Fauré's friend Charles Martin Loeffler had informed the Hills that a subscription to aid the needy composer might yield them a manuscript.

38 Georg Büchner, 1813–1837. *Wozzek.* Berlin and Charlottenburg, [1919]. ✦ Extensively revised in manuscript by Alban Berg as a preliminary draft of the libretto for his opera. From the collection of Louis Krasner, the American violinist who commissioned from Berg and premiered the violin concerto.

Purchased (1989) with the Amy Lowell fund.

39 Arnold Schönberg, 1874–1951. *Gurre-Lieder.* Leipzig and Vienna, 1912. ✦ Signed copy of the first edition, heavily marked up by Schönberg (in red pencil) and others, perhaps for performance. All the changes were adopted in the 1920 engraved edition. From the collection of Louis Krasner.

Acquired (1989) with funds given by Francis Goelet, H 1947, L 1952; Oscar S. Schafer, H 1961, MBA 1964; the Susan A. E. Morse fund; Mrs. Gardner Cox; Mrs. Otto Eckstein, R 1955; Peter J. Gellert, H 1947; Mr. and Mrs. Gordon P. Getty; the Oscar Handlin fund; the Byron S. Hurlbut Memorial fund; Robert H. Orchard, H 1942; Dr. Maurice M. Pechet, PhD 1944, MD 1948, and Mrs. Pechet; Charles I. Petschek, MBA 1948; Dr. Mark Ptashne, PhD 1968; and Anina Nitze Thompson. At the same time Louis Krasner's papers, from which this and the following item came, were presented by Mrs. Louis Krasner, Mrs. Naomi Orenstein, and Mrs. Elsa Miller.

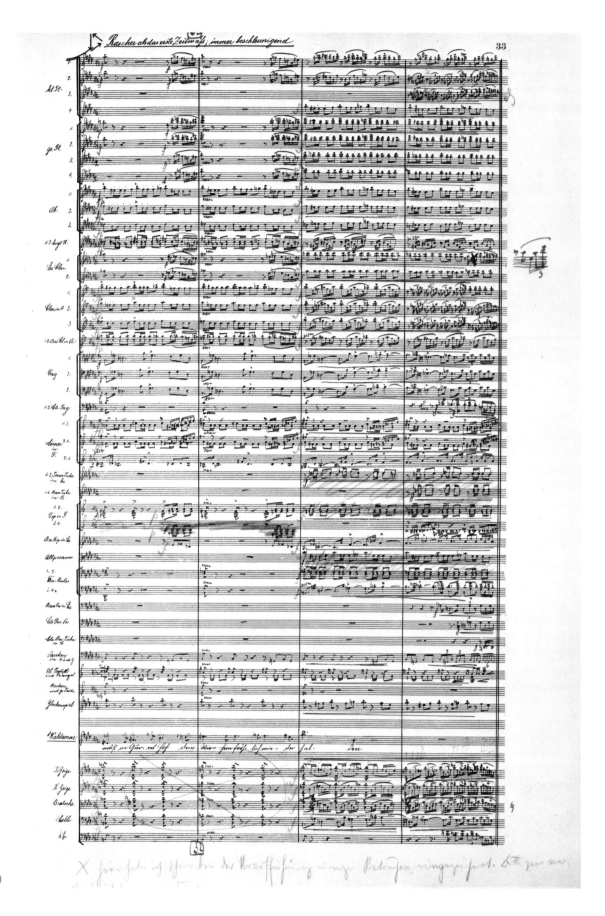

40 William Shakespeare, 1564–1616. *M. William Shak-speare: His true chronicle historie of the life and death of King Lear and his three daughters.* London, 1608. ◆ From the collection of William Augustus White, H 1863, who acquired it at the Mostyn sale in 1907. With White's annotation: "*By far* the finest copy in existence."

Given (1928–29) by members of the White family and other friends of the Harvard College Library, as part of a great gift of Elizabethan literature from W. A. White's collection.

41 William Shakespeare, 1564–1616. *The dramatic works.* Boston, 1837. ◆ Herman Melville's marked copy. Volume seven (including *King Lear*) was read and marked by Melville during the composition of *Moby Dick*. The curse on the harpoon in the Tryworks passage is written out in Melville's hand.

Acquired (1934) by gift of Eleanor Melville Metcalf and with income from the book fund given by Henry Saltonstall Howe, H 1869. Howe gave his library of association copies and a book fund to continue it. Mrs. Metcalf gave the J. O. Eaton portrait of Melville, the manuscripts of *Billy Budd* and the late poems, and other Melville items.

41

42 Miguel de Cervantes Saavedra, 1547–1616. *El ingenioso hidalgo Don Quixote de la Mancha.* Madrid, 1605, 1615. 2 vols. ◆ First edition of each volume, preliminaries of volume one in facsimile. From the collection of Templeton Crocker. Given

(1955) by Templeton Crocker's granddaughter, Mrs. Henry Potter Russell, in memory of Henry Potter Russell, Class of 1915.

Novelas exemplares. Madrid, 1613. ◆ Purchased (1948) with gifts from the Friends of the Harvard College Library, as an addition to the great Cervantes collection formed and given by Carl T. Keller, H 1894.

43 Pierre Corneille, 1606–1684. *Le Cid*. Paris, 1637. ◆ The second issue of the first edition, in contemporary vellum wrappers. *Le Cid* was written at a time when an influential movement in France attempted to regularize tragedy through the use of the "classical" unities of time, place, and action. First performed in 1637, it was an immediate popular success, soon marred by a literary quarrel fostered by jealous rivals. Eventually *Le Cid* was suppressed from public performance by Richelieu following the judgment of the Académie Française, which found the play "irregular," dramatically implausible, and morally weak. From the Charles W. Clark Collection.

Presented (1958) by Mrs. Imrie de Vegh from a collection of French literature purchased *en bloc* for Harvard by Imrie de Vegh and Curt H. Reisinger, H 1912.

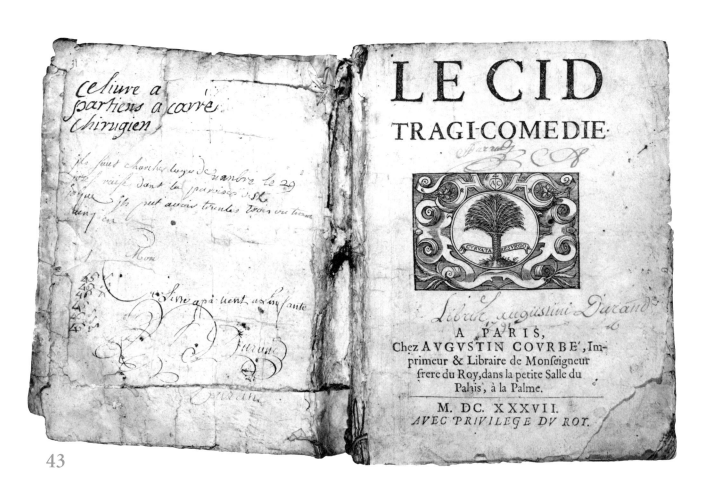

44 René Descartes, 1596–1650. *Discours de la méthode.* Leyden, 1637. • With the *Discours*, Descartes proposed a radically new way of acquiring knowledge based on the method of universal doubt. Just as Galileo wrote in the vernacular, so Descartes wrote the *Discours* in French so that all men and women of *bon sens* could learn to think for themselves and tell true from false by the natural light of reason.

Given (1919) by George Herbert Palmer, H 1864, who collected philosophy for Harvard and English poetry for Wellesley College.

45 Izaak Walton, 1593–1683. *The compleat angler or The contemplative man's recreation.* Copies of the first five editions: London, 1653, 1655, 1661, 1668, and 1676. • Bound as a matched set in green morocco, extra gilt, and boxed by Rivière & Son.

Given (1915) by Daniel B. Fearing, AM 1911 (honorary), whose great collection of Angling literature was accorded a separate classification in Widener Library.

46 Andrea Pozzo, 1642–1709. *Perspectiva pictorum et architectorum.* Rome, 1693–1700. 2 vols. • Fra Andrea's designs, widely circulated, became influential models for both church and theatre. Their stage-like quality, proscenium arches, and *quadratura* backdrops laid the foundations for eighteenth-century scenographic architecture.

Presented (1965) by Arthur and Charlotte Vershbow, R 1945, generous supporters of the Department of Printing and Graphic Arts in the Houghton Library. A selection from their private collection was exhibited at Houghton and described by David P. Becker in a catalogue entitled *Fact and fantasy* (1976).

47 Jean Baptiste Poquelin Molière, 1622–1673. *L'escole des maris.* Paris, 1661. • The sixth play of Molière, *L'escole des maris* opened at the Palais Royal on 24 June 1661. Molière took particular care with its publication. Angered by the fact that two of his previous plays had been pirated, he obtained a privilege for the work and entrusted its publication to Charles de Sercy, who shared it with four other printers. *L'escole des maris* was first published on 20 August 1661, its privilege identifying the imprimeur-libraire Ribou as perpetrator of the piracies. An engraved title-page shows Molière in the part of Sganarelle. From the Charles W. Clark Collection.

Presented (1956) by Curt H. Reisinger, H 1912.

46

48 Sir Isaac Newton, 1642–1727. *Philosophiae naturalis principia mathematica.* London, 1687. ❖ Copies of both issues of the first edition, each in its original calf binding. Celebrated for its exposition of the laws of motion and of universal gravitation, this is the most influential classic in all the literature of science.

Given (1991) by David P. Wheatland, H 1922.

49 Sébastien Rasles, 1657–1724. Dictionary of the Abnaki Language. Autograph MS., 1691, bound in 1842. ❖ "Taken after the fight at Norridgewalk, among Father Rasle's Papers and given by the late Col: Heath to Elisha Cooke Esqr." Published by John Pickering in the *Memoirs* of the American Academy (1833).

Given (1764) by Middlecott Cooke, H 1723. Cooke was one of those who helped to restore the College Library after the fire of 1764. Another of his gifts was a Bay Psalm Book, 1640.

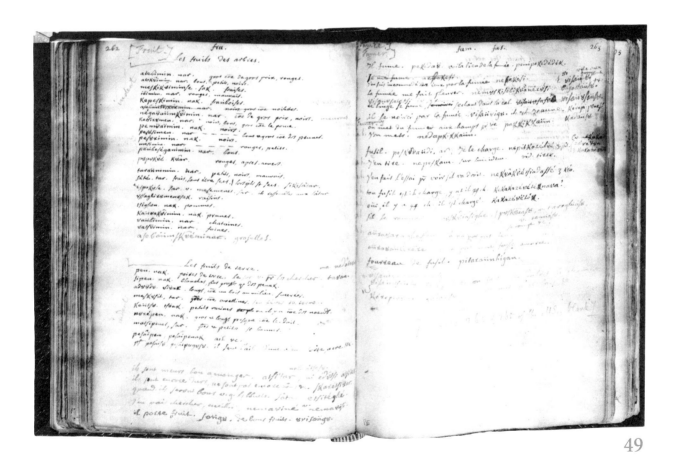

50   Giambattista Piranesi, 1720–1778. *Antichità romane de' tempi della Repubblica . . . Parte prima.* Rome, 1748.   •   Extremely rare as a separate volume, this first edition comprises twenty-eight engraved plates, most likely in an earlier state than the impressions found in the combined issue of 1750 entitled *Opere varie di architettura.*

Presented (1967) by Arthur and Charlotte Vershbow, R 1945.

51   Henry Fielding, 1707–1754. *Amelia.* London, 1752 [i.e. 1751]. 4 vols.   •   Fielding's least successful novel. This is the only known copy to contain the two sheets of an abortive second edition. Bound in contemporary full red morocco, gilt.

Given (1987) by the Viscountess Eccles, whose first husband, the late Donald F. Hyde, formed the extensive Fielding collection with which this book came to Harvard.

52   Paolo Posi, 1708–1776. *Prospetto della seconda machina rappresentante una Deliziosa all' uso cinese.* [Rome], 1760. 53 x 38 cm.   •   One of an extremely rare collection of 53 engravings depicting the festival known as the "Presentazione della Chinea." "Chinea" was the name given to the white horse presented each year in tribute

to the Pope by the King of Naples, from the tenth to the eighteenth century. In its last century, the festival developed into a popular two-day celebration, including fireworks. The construction of the elaborate "machines" was entrusted to the foremost architects and designers of the day, among whom was Paolo Posi. Posi's designs for the "presentazione" include some of the finest eighteenth-century decorations for fireworks display.

Purchased (1972) with funds presented by Franklin H. Kissner, H 1930, Honorary Curator of Roman Books, who established an endowment for the Houghton Library.

53   John Baskerville, 1706–1775. A specimen. [Birmingham, ca. 1762]. Broadside. 42 x 29.5 cm. • Baskerville came to type design free from the traditions of the type-founding or printing trades. A writing master, he paid attention to contemporary hands and was open to the influence of French experiments. Although his designs were not of great novelty, they marked a transition in England between old face and modern face. This is the first edition of Baskerville's specimen sheet with border of "lozenge and star." Only three copies are recorded.

Presented (1976) by William Bentinck-Smith, H 1937.

54   Cesare marchese di Beccaria, 1738–1794. *Dei delitti e delle pene.* [Livorno], 1764. • The first edition of Beccaria's celebrated work on the reform of criminal justice. Founded on the utilitarian principle that criminal policy should seek the greatest good for the greatest number, the *Dei delitti* condemned the brutal practices of the day and advocated penalties only severe enough to achieve order and security. Bound with this copy is Ferdinando Facchinei's *Note*, 1765, denouncing Beccaria's work for its socialistic tendencies.

Purchased (1980) with funds presented by Franklin H. Kissner, H 1930.

55   United States. *In Congress, July 4, 1776. A Declaration by the Representatives of the United States of America, in General Congress Assembled.* Philadelphia, 1776. Broadside. 45 x 38.5 cm. • First edition of the Declaration of Independence, one of twenty-five surviving copies.

Given (1947) by Carleton R. Richmond, H 1909, who formed and presented to the Library important collections of Samuel Pepys and John Evelyn.

In CONGRESS, July 4, 1776.

A DECLARATION

By the REPRESENTATIVES of the

UNITED STATES OF AMERICA,

In GENERAL CONGRESS ASSEMBLED.

WHEN in the Courfe of human Events, it becomes neceffary for one People to diffolve the Political Bands which have connected them with another, and to affume among the Powers of the Earth, the feparate and equal Station to which the Laws of Nature and of Nature's God entitle them, a decent Refpect to the Opinions of Mankind requires that they fhould declare the caufes which impel them to the Separation.

We hold thefe Truths to be felf-evident, that all Men are created equal, that they are endowed by their Creator with certain unalienable Rights, that among thefe are Life, Liberty, and the Purfuit of Happinefs—That to fecure thefe Rights, Governments are inftituted among Men, deriving their juft Powers from the Confent of the Governed, that whenever any Form of Government becomes deftructive of thefe Ends, it is the Right of the People to alter or to abolifh it, and to inftitute new Government, laying its Foundation on fuch Principles, and organizing its Powers in fuch Form, as to them fhall feem moft likely to effect their Safety and Happinefs. Prudence, indeed, will dictate that Governments long eftablifhed fhould not be changed for light and tranfient Caufes; and accordingly all Experience hath fhewn, that Mankind are more difpofed to fuffer, while Evils are fufferable, than to right themfelves by abolifhing the Forms to which they are accuftomed. But when a long Train of Abufes and Ufurpations, purfuing invariably the fame Object, evinces a Defign to reduce them under abfolute Defpotifm, it is their Right, it is their Duty, to throw off fuch Government, and to provide new Guards for their future Security. Such has been the patient Sufferance of thefe Colonies; and fuch is now the Neceffity which conftrains them to alter their former Syftems of Government. The Hiftory of the prefent King of Great-Britain is a Hiftory of repeated Injuries and Ufurpations, all having in direct Object the Eftablifhment of an abfolute Tyranny over thefe States. To prove this, let Facts be fubmitted to a candid World.

He has refufed his Affent to Laws, the moft wholefome and neceffary for the public Good.

He has forbidden his Governors to pafs Laws of immediate and preffing Importance, unlefs fufpended in their Operation till his Affent fhould be obtained; and when fo fufpended, he has utterly neglected to attend to them.

He has refufed to pafs other Laws for the Accommodation of large Diftricts of People, unlefs thofe People would relinquifh the Right of Reprefentation in the Legiflature, a Right ineftimable to them, and formidable to Tyrants only.

He has called together Legiflative Bodies at Places unufual, uncomfortable, and diftant from the Depofitory of their public Records, for the fole Purpofe of fatiguing them into Compliance with his Meafures.

He has diffolved Reprefentative Houfes repeatedly, for oppofing with manly Firmnefs his Invafions on the Rights of the People.

He has refufed for a long Time, after fuch Diffolutions, to caufe others to be elected; whereby the Legiflative Powers, incapable of Annihilation, have returned to the People at large for their exercife; the State remaining in the mean time expofed to all the Dangers of Invafion from without, and Convulfions within.

He has endeavoured to prevent the Population of thefe States; for that Purpofe obftructing the Laws for Naturalization of Foreigners; refufing to pafs others to encourage their Migrations hither, and raifing the Conditions of new Appropriations of Lands.

He has obftructed the Adminiftration of Juftice, by refufing his Affent to Laws for eftablifhing Judiciary Powers.

He has made Judges dependent on his Will alone, for the Tenure of their Offices, and the Amount and Payment of their Salaries.

He has erected a Multitude of new Offices, and fent hither Swarms of Officers to harrafs our People, and eat out their Subftance.

He has kept among us, in Times of Peace, Standing Armies, without the confent of our Legiflatures.

He has affected to render the Military independent of and fuperior to the Civil Power.

He has combined with others to fubject us to a Jurifdiction foreign to our Conftitution, and unacknowledged by our Laws; giving his Affent to their Acts of pretended Legiflation:

For quartering large Bodies of Armed Troops among us:

For protecting them, by a mock Trial, from Punifhment for any Murders which they fhould commit on the Inhabitants of thefe States:

For cutting off our Trade with all Parts of the World:

For impofing Taxes on us without our Confent:

For depriving us, in many Cafes, of the Benefits of Trial by Jury:

For tranfporting us beyond Seas to be tried for pretended Offences:

For abolifhing the free Syftem of Englifh Laws in a neighbouring Province, eftablifhing therein an arbitrary Government, and enlarging its Boundaries, fo as to render it at once an Example and fit Inftrument for introducing the fame abfolute Rule into thefe Colonies:

For taking away our Charters, abolifhing our moft valuable Laws, and altering fundamentally the Forms of our Governments:

For fufpending our own Legiflatures, and declaring themfelves invefted with Power to legiflate for us in all Cafes whatfoever.

He has abdicated Government here, by declaring us out of his Protection and waging War againft us.

He has plundered our Seas, ravaged our Coafts, burnt our Towns, and deftroyed the Lives of our People.

He is, at this Time, tranfporting large Armies of foreign Mercenaries to compleat the Works of Death, Defolation, and Tyranny, already begun with circumftances of Cruelty and Perfidy, fcarcely paralleled in the moft barbarous Ages, and totally unworthy the Head of a civilized Nation.

He has conftrained our fellow Citizens taken Captive on the high Seas to bear Arms againft their Country, to become the Executioners of their Friends and Brethren, or to fall themfelves by their Hands.

He has excited domeftic Infurrections amongft us, and has endeavoured to bring on the Inhabitants of our Frontiers, the mercilefs Indian Savages, whofe known Rule of Warfare, is an undiftinguifhed Deftruction, of all Ages, Sexes and Conditions.

In every ftage of thefe Oppreffions we have Petitioned for Redrefs in the moft humble Terms: Our repeated Petitions have been anfwered only by repeated Injury. A Prince, whofe Character is thus marked by every act which may define a Tyrant, is unfit to be the Ruler of a free People.

Nor have we been wanting in Attentions to our Britifh Brethren. We have warned them from Time to Time of Attempts by their Legiflature to extend an unwarrantable Jurifdiction over us. We have reminded them of the Circumftances of our Emigration and Settlement here. We have appealed to their native Juftice and Magnanimity, and we have conjured them by the Ties of our common Kindred to difavow thefe Ufurpations, which, would inevitably interrupt our Connections and Correfpondence. They too have been deaf to the Voice of Juftice and of Confanguinity. We muft, therefore, acquiefce in the Neceffity, which denounces our Separation, and hold them, as we hold the reft of Mankind, Enemies in War, in Peace, Friends.

We, therefore, the Reprefentatives of the UNITED STATES OF AMERICA, in General Congress, Affembled, appealing to the Supreme Judge of the World for the Rectitude of our Intentions, do, in the Name, and by Authority of the good People of thefe Colonies, folemnly Publifh and Declare, That thefe United Colonies are, and of Right ought to be, FREE AND INDEPENDENT STATES; that they are abfolved from all Allegiance to the Britifh Crown, and that all political Connection between them and the State of Great-Britain, is and ought to be totally diffolved; and that as FREE AND INDEPENDENT STATES, they have full Power to levy War, conclude Peace, contract Alliances, eftablifh Commerce, and to do all other Acts and Things which INDEPENDENT STATES may of right do. And for the fupport of this Declaration, with a firm Reliance on the Protection of divine Providence, we mutually pledge to each other our Lives, our Fortunes, and our facred Honor.

Signed by ORDER *and in* BEHALF *of the* CONGRESS,

JOHN HANCOCK, President.

ATTEST.
CHARLES THOMSON, Secretary.

PHILADELPHIA: PRINTED BY JOHN DUNLAP.

56 Antonio Allegri Correggio, 1489?–1534. *Pitture di . . . Correggio esistenti in Parma nel monistero di San Paolo.* Parma, co' tipi Bodoniani, 1800. ✦ Bodoni chose to print the *Pitture* on his own press to celebrate the recent union of Don Lodovico, Prince of Parma, with the Infanta of Spain, Maria Luigia. G. G. Rossi's Italian introduction, translated into French and Spanish, allowed Bodoni to demonstrate his typographic virtuosity, while the plates, engraved with the greatest care by Francesco Rosaspina, reproduced one of the treasures of the city of Parma, Correggio's convent ceiling of S. Paolo, executed ca. 1519.

Presented (1964) by Ward M. Canaday, H 1907, and Mrs. Canaday.

57 Remondini (Firm). *Campione delle carte colorate della fabbrica.* Bassano, 1808. ✦ One of twenty-four sample books of decorated papers, 1790–1852, from the firm of Giuseppe Remondini e figli in Bassano.

Purchased (1967) with funds presented by Augustus P. Loring, H 1938, MBA 1940, and with income from the Rosamond B. Loring fund, established by Augustus P. Loring, H 1908, in memory of his wife. Rosamond Loring, paper artist, collector, and author of *Decorated book papers* (1942, 1952) bequeathed (1951) samples of her own work in addition to her collection of books and pamphlets illustrating the history and techniques of decorated paper.

58 [Petrus Peregrinus, Maricurtensis, 13th century]. *Raymundus Lulius De Virtute Magnetis.* [Rome, 1520]. ✦ Hans Christian Oersted, 1777–1851. *Experimenta circa effectum conflictus electrici in acum magneticam.* [Copenhagen, 1820]. ✦

First account of the magnet (loadstone) and its poles, together with Oersted's announcement of his discovery of electromagnetism by demonstrating that electric currents cause a magnetic field. These are the key works in the Wheatland collection of books on electricity.

Given (1991) by David P. Wheatland, ʜ 1922.

59

59 Eugène Delacroix, 1798–1863. Study for the Duel of Faust and Valentin, an illustration to Johann Wolfgang von Goethe, *Faust*, Paris, 1828. Pen and brown ink on wove paper. 30 x 23.5 cm. ◆ Delacroix's daring lithographs demonstrated that a modern book could be a work of art. It is the first livre d'artiste.

Presented (1979) by David P. Becker in honor of Eleanor M. Garvey, Philip Hofer Curator of Printing and Graphic Arts, Emerita.

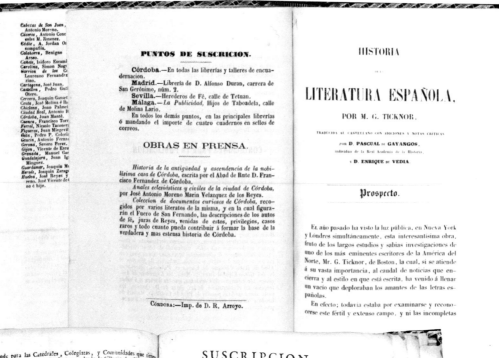

60 Selections from a collection of some four hundred Spanish prospectuses for books and periodicals printed between 1780 and 1860, largely in Madrid. Collected by Vicente Castañeda y Alcover and bound in four volumes. Types, illustrations, and sample pages are shown in this remarkable assemblage of the ephemera of Spanish subscription publication.

Purchased (1983) with income from the fund established by Mary P. C. Nash in memory of her husband, Bennett Hubbard Nash, H 1856, for the purchase of Spanish and Italian books.

61 John Palfrey, 1768–1843. MS. Journal and Cotton Book. Attakapis, La., 1807–14. ⬩ Includes lists of slaves and daily records of their productivity, "Accot. of Cotton pick'd in Crop of 1812." When the Abolitionist J. G. Palfrey inherited the property, he freed its slaves and sold it off.

Given (1941) with the Palfrey Papers by Dr. James B. Ayer, H 1903, and Mrs. Ayer.

62 William Henry Fox Talbot, 1800–1877. *Sun pictures in Scotland.* London, 1845. ⬩ Talbot's second photographically illustrated book contains two letterpress leaves and twenty-three calotypes representing Abbotsford and other "Scenes connected with the life and writings of Sir Walter Scott." Talbot's process used here and in *The pencil of nature* of 1844 proved superior to the daguerreotype as it allowed the negative image to be reproduced on paper any number of times. Some 118 copies were painstakingly produced for the benefit of aristocratic subscribers, among whom were Queen Victoria, the Duchess of Kent, and the Duke of Devonshire.

Given (1982) by Harrison D. Horblit, H 1933, MBA 1936.

63 Dorothea Lynde Dix, 1802–1887. Report [of] the committee to which was referred the subject of a Hospital for the insane poor of this Commonwealth. [Pennsylvania, n.d.]. ⬩ One of numerous MS. reports and appeals composed and circulated by Dix in her incessant attempts to improve conditions and provide facilities for the insane. Daguerreotype portrait. Mat signed "M. A. Root, 140 Chestnut St., Philada."

Given with Dorothea Dix's papers (1938) by Mrs. Horatio A. Lamb.

64 Edward Lear, 1812–1888. Thirty-eight original drawings for *A book of nonsense.* Pen and ink drawings with autograph limericks, mounted on cardboard sheets measuring 20 x 17 cm. ⬩ First published in *A book of nonsense*, third edition, London, 1861.

Given (1942) by William B. Osgood Field, who was encouraged to collect the drawings and books of Edward Lear by Houghton's first Curator of Printing and Graphic Arts, Philip Hofer. Field also collected material by John Leech and other English illustrators. A portion of his vast collection is listed in his two books, *John Leech on my shelves* (1930) and *Edward Lear on my shelves* (1933). His gift of more than three thousand books and drawings gave the Houghton Library an unrivalled Edward Lear collection.

97

There was a young lady of Ryde,
Whose shoestrings were seldom untied:
She purchased some clogs, and some small spotty dogs,
And frequently walked about Ryde.

65 Lewis Carroll, 1832–1898. *Alice's adventures in Wonderland . . . With forty-two illustrations by John Tenniel.* London, 1865. ◆ The author's own copy, bound for him in gilt vellum, all edges gilt, Alice on the upper cover and the Cheshire cat on the lower. Intended for presentation to Alice Liddell, on the third anniversary of their river excursion, but returned to the author when the edition was withdrawn. Only twenty-three copies of the first edition survive. From the collections of G. M. Williamson and Harcourt Amory, H 1876.

Given (1927) by Mrs. Harcourt Amory together with her husband's rich collection of first editions, MSS., and Carrolliana.

66 Julia Margaret Cameron, 1815–1879. *Illustrations to Tennyson's Idylls of the King, and other poems.* London, 1875. 2 vols. ◆ Starting in 1863 Julia Cameron photographed the members of her circle, including Tennyson, Darwin, Carlyle, and Browning. In 1874, Tennyson asked her to create illustrations for his *Idylls of the*

King. She posed and costumed models, preparing twenty-six subjects from glass negatives by the wet-collodion process. Two photographs of Tennyson in the garb of a monk serve as frontispieces.

Purchased (v. 1, 1943; v. 2, 1968) with income from the Frank B. Bemis fund, and from the Hugh Gray Lieber fund, Charles Eliot Norton fund, and Sarah Norton bequest fund.

67 Sarah Wyman Whitman, 1842–1902. Sketchbook. [Boston], ca. 1885. ✦ Sarah Whitman studied art with William Morris Hunt and Thomas Couture. An accomplished draughtswoman, she became a designer of book covers for Houghton, Mifflin & Co. in 1880, and began designing for stained glass about 1885. This sketchbook reveals her activity in both areas. It includes, among other drawings and notations, a pencil design for the cover of *A marsh island* by Sarah Orne Jewett (Boston, 1885), one of six covers Whitman designed for Jewett's books.

Bequeathed (1982) by Margaret T. Clark, courtesy of Mrs. Daniel S. Grosch.

67

68 Geoffrey Chaucer, d. 1400. *The works of Geoffrey Chaucer.* Hammersmith, 1896. ✦ The crowning achievement of the Kelmscott Press. The publication of the works of Chaucer was discussed as early as 1850 by William Morris and Edward Burne-Jones when they "discovered" Chaucer while at Oxford. The actual project, begun in 1892, required the design and casting of a new type, over eighty illustrations by

Edward Burne-Jones, a decorated title-page, and a number of borders and initials by William Morris. This is one of thirteen copies printed on vellum and one of forty-eight bound in a full white pigskin binding executed at the Doves bindery from Morris's design.

Presented (1906) by Henry Arthur Jones, н 1907 (honorary), playwright and drama critic.

69 Hugo von Hofmannsthal, 1874–1929. *Gestern. Studie in einem Akt, in Reimen.* Wien, 1891. ◆ The author's first book, published under the pseudonym Theophil Morren and inscribed under that name to Richard Beer-Hofmann. This short verse drama prefigures Hofmannsthal's later masterworks.

Bequeathed (1986) by Eugene M. Weber, PhD 1966, editor and collector of Hofmannsthal's work.

mon ami et cher confrère,
en mettant dans vos mains cette
petite scènette, ces mannequins
encore humides et couverts de
couleurs criardes, qui me font mal,
j'agis bien en égoïste. Nous
en causerons, un jour Et c'est alors
que j'espère les reprendre, reluisants
du vermeil de votre esprit et
gracieuses comme des pouppées
de Saxe.
Théophil Morren
Décembre 91.

Theophil Morren.

Gestern.

Studie in einem Akt, in Reimen.

Den Bühnen gegenüber als Manuskript gedruckt.

Wien 1891.
Verlag der „Modernen Rundschau".

70   *The Yellow Kid* 1–9 (March 20–July 17, 1897). ◆   Humor magazine, progenitor of the pulp comics. The Kid was drawn by R. F. Outcault.

Purchased (1959) with income from the fund established in memory of Caroline Miller Parker, whose splendid collections of Randolph Caldecott and Walter Crane were given by Augustin H. Parker, H 1897. Mr. Parker gave to the Library his own collection of Oliver Goldsmith, as well as acquisition funds for his own and his wife's collections.

71   Frank Lloyd Wright, 1867–1959. *Ausgeführte Bauten und Entwürfe.* [Berlin, E. Wasmuth, 1910].   •   One of the key works in the history of modern architecture and a tour de force in fine printing. The two portfolios illustrate some seventy buildings from the period 1893 to 1909. They include seventy-two plates with twenty-eight tissue overlays, which Wright and two assistants traced in size and scale. The first edition exists in two states, the present one being preferable as it is printed on japanese paper, with overlays on india paper. There were one thousand copies, five hundred of which, intended for American distribution, were burned or water-damaged in a fire at Taliesin.

Presented (1973) by Philip Hofer, H 1921, LHD 1967, in honor of Fernando Zóbel de Ayala, H 1949, L 1958, sometime apprentice in the Department of Printing and Graphic Arts. An artist himself, Zóbel founded the modern art museum at Cuenca.

72   Boris Leonidovich Pasternak, 1890–1960. *Bliznets v' Tuchakh': Stikhi.* Moskva, 1914.   •   The poet's first book, a collection of poems in original printed wrappers. The only copy in America.

Purchased (1989) with income from the book fund established by Bayard L. Kilgour Jr., H 1927, who founded at Harvard the greatest collection of Russian literature in the West.

73   Fernando Pessoa, 1888–1935. *35 sonnets.* Lisbon, 1918.   •   *Antinous, a poem.* Lisbon, 1918.   •   *English poems I-II.* Lisbon, 1921.   •   *English poems III.* Lisbon, 1921.   •   *Mensagem.* Lisbon, 1934.   •   A complete set of first editions, all in printed wrappers, unbound, the last inscribed to José Osorio de Oliveira. Many consider Pessoa the only rival to Camões in all of Portuguese literature.

Purchased (1988–89) with income from the Amy Lowell fund.

74   Marcus Garvey, 1887–1940. *Aims and objects of movement for solution of negro problem outlined . . . Help negroes to have a nation of their own in Africa.* New York, 1924.   •   Platform of the Universal Negro Improvement Association, which exalted Black people but, frustrated by American society, called for a return to Africa.

Purchased (1969) with income from the book fund established by Charles Warren, H 1889, historian of the Supreme Court, who established endowments for American history, for library acquisitions, and for a curatorship.

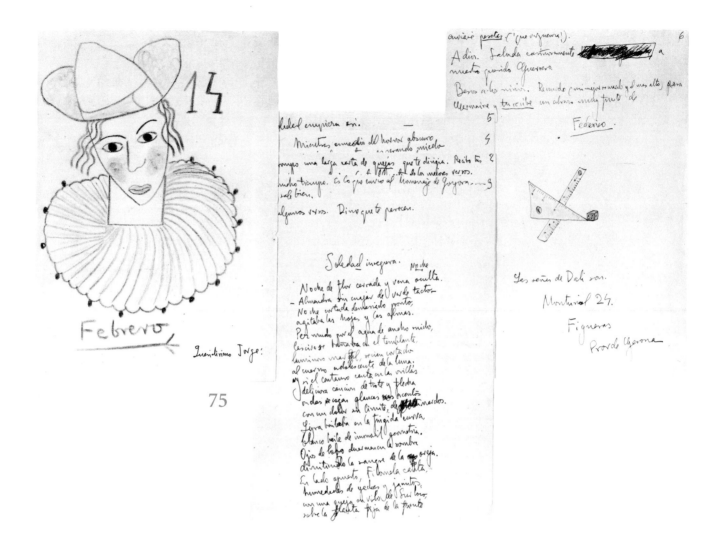

75

75 Federico García Lorca, 1898–1936. Autograph letter, signed, to Jorge Guillén, with original drawing of a Pierrot's head in colored pencil. [Granada?], 14 February [1927]. 6 leaves. 16 x 22.5 cm. ◆ Part of an important series of letters sent by Lorca to Jorge Guillén, together with drafts of poems and original drawings from the period 1925–28. Many of the letters were published in Guillén's *Federico en persona, semblanza y epistolario* (1959).

Presented (1985) by Claudio Guillén, AM 1947, PhD 1953, and Teresa Guillén Gilman as part of a large collection of their father's work. The Guillén papers, together with those of Pedro Salinas, given (1975) by Mrs. Jaime Pedro Salinas and Mrs. Solita Salinas de Marichal, form at Houghton an outstanding collection of the members of the Generation of 1927, who dominated Spanish letters in the decade preceding the Civil War.

76   Julia Peterkin, 1880–1961. *Roll, Jordan, roll.* New York, 1933.   •   Peterkin's essays on Southern life are illustrated with a frontispiece and ninety photo-engraved plates by Doris Ulmann (1884–1934), who began her photographic career as a portraitist in 1918 and, from 1925 on, spent half of each year on the road documenting Black life in the South with her camera.

Given (1936) by Mrs. Henry Necarsulmer in memory of her sister Doris Ulmann.

77 Rosamond Bowditch Loring, 1889–1950. Tools for decorating paper. [1930–40]. ❖ Combs and rolling pins, hand-made or adapted by Rosamond Loring for her use in the making of paste or marbled paper.

Bequeathed (1951) by Rosamond B. Loring.

78

78 Ben Shahn, 1898–1969. *A bestiary for Moncha.* [Cambridge, Mass., 1957]. •
Pen and black ink on wove paper. 7 x 4.5 cm. Ben Shahn, then Norton
Professor at Harvard, drew this bestiary for Moncha, wife of his friend José Luis Sert. It
consists of twelve original drawings of animals with a calligraphic cover, the whole
inserted in a small silver box decorated with beasts in repoussé. Later adapted as illustrations for an edition of Christopher Smart's *Jubilate Agno,* printed for the Fogg Art
Museum in 1957.

Presented (1982) by Professor José Luis Sert, AM 1953 (honorary), and Mrs. Sert.

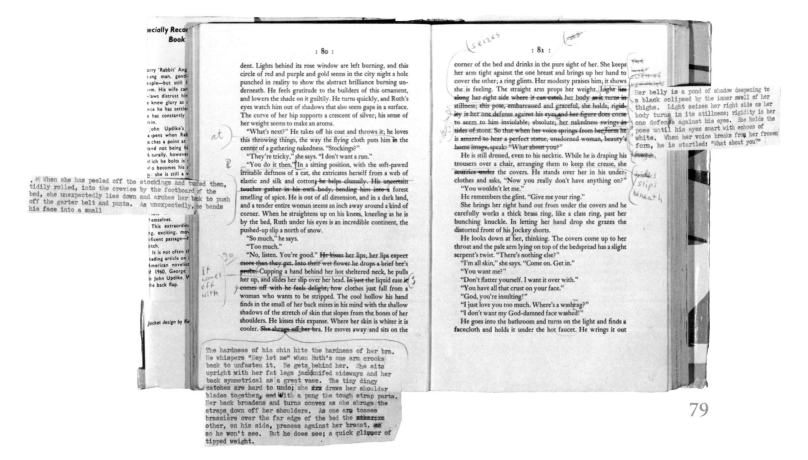

79 John Updike, b. 1932. *Rabbit, run.* London, 1961. • The author's copy of the André Deutsch edition, extensively revised in ink and with typed slips pasted on in preparation for the London Penguin edition of 1964. Some of the additions to the text of the Penguin edition come from previously unprinted portions of the original draft.

Presented (1969) by John Updike, н 1954, who, beginning in 1966, has given to or deposited at Houghton all his manuscripts and correspondence. In 1987 he wrote an introduction to the Library's catalogue of an exhibition based on his collection, *The art of adding and the art of taking away*, and spoke at a symposium marking the exhibition opening.

80 Josef Albers, 1888–1976. *Interaction of colour.* New Haven and London, 1963. 3 parts in a case. • A born educator, Josef Albers experimented with participatory teaching methods in his native Germany from his early days as a public school art teacher through his years at the Bauhaus. After emigrating to this country, he

continued to develop special classes in basic drawing and color, particularly during his years at Yale in the fifties and early sixties. The *Interaction of colour* is the result of his and his students' reflections. This is the first edition, designed by Norman Ives and printed by Carl Purington Rollins at the Printing Office of the Yale University Press.

Presented (1977) by Fernando Zóbel de Ayala, ʜ 1949, ʟ 1958, whose generous gifts of Spanish literature and of art have greatly enriched the library's collection in these fields.

81 Jorge Luis Borges, 1899–1986. *El otro.* Buenos Aires, 1972. ◆ One of fifty-seven copies, illustrated with two etchings of the Charles River bank by Ana Maria Moncalvo, and published on Borges's birthday. The author, Charles Eliot Norton Lecturer at Harvard in 1967–68, describes himself sitting on a bench by the Charles River in Cambridge, 1969, encountering his younger self sitting on a bench by the River Rhône in Geneva, 1918. Conversation between the Doubles turns on the future of Argentinian culture and dissolves in the confusing realities of the two "caricatures." The story was collected in *The book of sand,* 1977.

Purchased (1989) with funds given by David A. Goldberg, ʜ 1954, ᴊᴅ 1957.

82 Václav Havel, b. 1936. *Audience (jednoaktová hra).* [Prague, Edice Petlice no. 47], 1975. ◆ Carbon-copy typescript in cardboard wrappers, cloth shelfback, signed by the author. First of the plays to feature Ferdinand Vaněk, generic dissident and alter-ego of the author. Vaněk was adopted by other playwrights and celebrated in the personal column of a Prague newspaper.

Purchased (1977) with income from the Milada Součková fund. Altogether the Library has collected some seven hundred unofficial Czech publications since 1973.

83 Samuel Beckett, 1906–1989. *Foirades/fizzles.* London, New York, 1976. ◆ Limited edition of 250. Five texts by Beckett and thirty-three etchings by Jasper Johns. Author and illustrator jointly explore the themes of identity and of illusion versus reality.

Presented (1978) by Richard M. Hunt, PhD 1960; William Bentinck-Smith, ʜ 1937; Mrs. Frederick Deknatel; David P. Becker; Lammot du Pont Copeland, ʜ 1928; Robert D. Graff, ʜ 1941, and Mrs. Graff.

84 Alexander Pope, 1688–1744. *Ethic epistles.* Autograph MS. of the first three books of *An essay on man*, laid out in imitation of print, with revisions and corrections. ✦ A perfect demonstration of literary composition articulated with typographic fashion. From the collection of Jerome Kern.

Given (1943) by Harold T. White, H 1897; William King Richardson, H 1880; Carleton R. Richmond, H 1909, and others.

85 Henry Fielding, 1707–1754. "Of Outlawry." Autograph MS. ✦ Fielding's largest surviving literary manuscript, from an *Institute of the pleas of the Crown* that he advertised in 1745 but never published. This and other fragments—including the table of contents, also at Harvard—were sold on the autograph market in the 1820s by Fielding's grandson, William Henry. From the collection of Donald F. Hyde.

Given (1987) by the Viscountess Eccles, Honorary Curator of English Literature and donor of the Donald F. Hyde Memorial Rooms in Houghton Library.

86 Benedict Arnold, 1741–1801. Journal of the Expedition against Quebec, September 27–October 30, 1775. Autograph MS. ✦ Starting from Cambridge with 1,100 men, Arnold led his forces by way of the Kennebec and Chaudière rivers in an enterprise which has been likened to Hannibal's crossing the Alps. Overcoming desertions and great hardships the gallant Arnold attacked and besieged the city. The journal is only partly published. From the collection of S.L.M. Barlow.

Given (1970) by Alfred C. Berol, H 1913, collector of Victorian literature, who gave to Harvard several important historical manuscripts.

87 Benjamin Robert Haydon, 1786–1846. Volume nine from the Diary. Autograph MS., 1810–20. ✦ Comprises, complete, thirty large volumes, one notebook, one genealogical scrapbook, and an incomplete autobiographical manuscript plus nearly two thousand letters. The text of the Diary was published by Harvard University Press (1960–63) in five volumes, edited by W. B. Pope. The artist Haydon met, conversed with, or corresponded with many of the important creative figures of his day, from Goethe to his friend Keats.

Given (1977) by Willard Bissell Pope, PhD 1932, together with a fund for further acquisition in memory of his wife Evelyn Ryan Pope.

Chap. 6. Of Outlawry in Criminal
Causes.

1. Upon an Indictment or appeal for Treason, Felony,
or Trespass, if the Deft be not in custody, a process
of Outlawry lies. But if he be
once in Custody of Record, as where the Sheriff returns
(2) copi to the Capias, if he afterwards Escape, the Sheriff
shall be punished, but no Exigent awarded (a) †

† This refers to ye fifth
page back

2. In order to prosecute a Criminal to an Outlawry there must
be either first an Appeal by the Party injured which was
formerly usual in all but which hath of late
been totally discontinued unless in rely. or 2dly
an Indictment
of Record in the Court whence
the Writ issues (b)
Ɵ This refers to ye fifth page back

3. If an Indictment be found in B.R. or removed into
that Court by Certiorari, a Capias issues to the Sheriff
of the County where the Deft is indicted, and on the Sheriff's
Return that he is not found in his Bailywick
an Exigent shall go unless it to testified
that the Deft is in some other County, then a Capias shall
issue into that County, and (c)

4. Justices of Oyer and Terminer may a Capias & Exigent
& so proceed to outlaw any person indicted before them. This

(1) The Reason of this is that no averment is suffered agt the truth of a Record. (2) Where a Sheriff arrest
a Man on a Writ the endorses on the Back of it copi corpus I have taken the Body, and at
Day or of Writ is returnable he Reads it Each where of Endorsement or Return
of the Sheriff become Records part of the Record. (3) The Writ commanding him to arrest
the Body is where is explained a little after. (5) An action Appeal ie a Call. or from whence
in the Civil Law and where a calling another to answer some allegation in a Court of Justice where
the plaintiff or caller is named Appellant, the Deft or person called on is the Appellee (6) of redress on

85

88 Percy Bysshe Shelley, 1792–1822. ◆ *To Constantia & other poems*. Autograph MS, 1817. The smaller, fair-copy notebook. Inscribed with notes about Shelley by Claire Clairmont and Edward A. Silsbee.

Bequeathed (1902) together with the larger notebook—fictionalized object of Henry James's *Aspern papers*—by Edward A. Silsbee, who travelled twice to Florence to visit Claire Clairmont's home in search of Shelley relics.

89 John Keats, 1795–1821. *Lamia*, 1820. ◆ Two leaves, of the autograph MS. draft and the proofs, corrected by Keats and annotated by Richard Woodhouse.

Given (1970) by Arthur A. Houghton Jr., H 1929, who built—and helped to renovate—Houghton Library, where his unrivalled Keats collection occupies a special exhibition room.

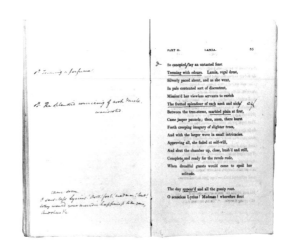

89

90 Georg Wilhelm Friedrich Hegel, 1770–1831. Autograph MS. ◆ Drafts of philosophical papers, aphorisms, notes for lectures, and retained copies of letters.

Purchased (1910) with funds contributed anonymously, an acquisition negotiated with Arnold Genthe by George Herbert Palmer, H 1864.

91 Edgar Allan Poe, 1809–1849. *The haunted palace.* Autograph MS., two pages, 1840? ◆ First written as part of Poe's tale, "The fall of the house of Usher," the poem is inscribed here in revised form. From the collection of R. W. Griswold, Poe's editor.

Given (1916) by Mrs. Murray Anthony Potter, Merrill Griswold, H 1907, and Mrs. Arthur W. Fletcher—descendants of R. W. Griswold, whose Poe manuscripts they gave to Harvard over many years.

92 Ralph Waldo Emerson, 1803–1882. Journal: Margaret Fuller Ossoli. Autograph MS., 1850–51. ◆ Notes gathered in preparation for *Memorials of Margaret Fuller*, 1852, edited by Emerson, J. F. Clarke, and W. H. Channing.

Given (1991) by the Ralph Waldo Emerson Memorial Association, with Emerson's complete Journals (in 197 volumes).

93 Henry Wadsworth Longfellow, 1807–1882. *The song of Hiawatha. First draft.* 1854–55. ◆ Autograph MS. in pencil, bound for Longfellow in half green calf, marbled boards. Revisions and corrections reveal, among other things, that the hero's name was originally Manabozha.

Purchased (1976) from the Longfellow House Trust.

94 Ticknor and Fields. MS. contract for the publication of *Walden*, signed by H. D. Thoreau and William D. Ticknor and Co., March 16, 1854. ◆ On the edition of two thousand copies Thoreau was to receive a royalty of fifteen percent of the retail price paid biannually, twenty-five copies, and a twenty-five percent discount for additional copies.

Rough cost book, 1852–54, containing entries for *Walden* and *The scarlet letter.*

"Pleasant is the sound," he answered,
"Pleasant is the voice that calls me!"

p.3.

Sternly then said old Nokomis
"Bring not here an idle maiden,
Bring not here a useless woman,
Hands unskilful, feet unwilling,
Bring a wife with nimble fingers,
Heart and hand that move together,
Feet that run on willing errands!"
Smiling answered Hiawatha,

On the outskirts of the forest,
'Twixt the shadow and the sunshine,
Herds of fallow deer were feeding,
But they saw not Hiawatha.
To his bow he whispered "Fail not!"
Whispered to his arrow "Swerve not!"
Sent it singing on its errand,
To the red heart of the roebuck;
Threw the deer across his shoulder,
And sped forward without pausing.

At the doorway of his wigwam
Sat the ancient Arrow-maker,
In the land of the Dacotahs,
Making arrow-heads of flint-stone,
Arrow-heads of chalcedony.
At his side, in all her beauty,
Sat the lovely Minnehaka,
Sat his daughter, Laughing Water,
Plaiting mats of flags and rushes.
Of the past the old man's thoughts were,
And the maiden's of the future.

Feb. 24. 55

93

This Indenture, of two parts, made
this sixteenth day of March in the
of our Lord, Eighteen hundred and
fifty five, by and between Henry
D. Thoreau of Concord in the County
of Middlesex and State of Massachusetts, of the first part, and William
D. Ticknor, John Reed Jr., and James
T. Fields of Boston, Booksellers and
Copartners under the firm of William
D. Ticknor and Co. of the second part.
Witnesseth, That the said Thoreau
agrees to give, and does by these presents
give to the said Ticknor & Co. the right
to publish, for the term of five years, a
certain book entitled "Walden, a
Life in the Woods." of which said Thoreau
is the Author and Proprietor.
And in consideration of the premises the
said Ticknor & Co. on their part agree
to cause said work to be printed, and
to publish at once an Edition of Two
Thousand copies, and to pay to the said
Thoreau, his heirs and assigns, fifteen
per cent on the retail price of said work

94

Given (1991) by the Houghton Mifflin Co. as part of its papers, which document 150 years of publishing by the oldest, and one of most distinguished publishing houses in this country.

95   Nathaniel Hawthorne, 1804–1864. *The house of the seven gables, a romance.* 1851.   ❖   Autograph MS. in ink, with some corrections and revisions.

Given (1915) by Mrs. James T. Fields. Her husband, who published the work, inscribed this manuscript "Copy sent by the author to the printer."

95

96 John Stuart Mill, 1806–1873. Various undated autograph MSS.: reviews, papers, critiques, etc. ◆ From the library of J. S. Mill, sold at Avignon in 1905.

Given (1919) by George Herbert Palmer, H 1864.

97 George Eliot, 1819–1880. *Quarry for Middlemarch.* Autograph MS. in a pocket notebook. 1869–72. ◆ Reading notes, time sequences, maps, and plot lines, integrating the two strands of the story into an eight-part serial.

Bequeathed (1925) by Amy Lowell.

98 Ferdinand de Saussure, 1857–1913. *Essai pour réduire les mots du Grec, du Latin et de l'Allemand à un petit nombre de racines.* Autograph MS. • The reportedly lost essay, referred to as an "enfantillage" in Saussure's *Souvenirs* (1959). Composed in 1872 when the boy was only fifteen years old, the *Essai* prefigured some important developments in Saussure's later work.

Purchased (1968) from the family as part of a collection of Saussure's manuscripts, with funds provided by the Friends of the Harvard College Library. Houghton's holdings, together with the Saussurian archive in the Bibliothèque Publique et Universitaire de Genève, form an invaluable source for the study of Saussure's legacy.

99 William James, 1842–1910. *The varieties of religious experience*, chapters 19 and 20. Autograph MS. and typescript, revised in manuscript, mounted in a notebook, 1902. ◆ Only these final parts of James's manuscript have survived. These papers served as printer's copy before James assembled them for oral delivery at the conclusion of his Gifford Lectures on Natural Religion at Edinburgh University in 1901–1902. Enthusiastically received in the lecture hall and in print, James's study continues to hold its own as the classic description of the essential facts.

Given (1928) by the James family, donors over the years of thousands of letters and MSS. of Alice, Henry, and William James.

100 Thomas Wolfe, 1900–1938. *O lost.* Autograph MS. in a ledger book, 1926. ◆ First draft of *Look homeward, angel*, composed in a London bedsitter, far from the home, family, and neighbors of Asheville, N.C., which Wolfe memorialized in his first novel.

Given (1939) in memory of William James by Gabriel Wells, bookseller and collector of New York City. The manuscript proved to be the magnet for the vast majority of Wolfe's papers that were presented to the library eight years later by William B. Wisdom, Jr.

101 George Bataille, 1897–1962. *Le bleu du ciel.* Autograph MSS., 1929–35. ◆ Written for the most part in 1935, *Le bleu du ciel* explores through the themes of sexuality and violence, perversion and political powerlessness, the ambivalent attitude of French intellectuals in the early 1930s. As such, it forms a pendant to Louis Ferdinand Céline's *Voyage au bout de la nuit* (1931) and André Malraux's *La condition humaine* (1933). This manuscript, a working draft, differs throughout from the published text, and includes an early version of "Dirty," dated 1929 in Bataille's hand.

Purchased (1985) with the Amy Lowell fund.

102 Leon Trotsky, 1879–1940. Stalin, an Appraisal of the Man and his Influence. Typescript and MS., 1940.

Purchased (1940) with funds presented by John W. Blodgett Jr., H 1923, generous Harvard benefactor for whom the Blodgett Court of Pusey Library is named. The purchase of the papers was negotiated with Trotsky before his assassination. Accompanying the manuscripts of Trotsky's works is his extensive correspondence.

2,550 copies of this book have been printed at
The Stinehour Press, in the Northeast Kingdom, at Lunenburg, Vermont.
Design and production have been carried out on a Macintosh computer
by Roderick Stinehour.
The types used are from Adobe Systems; *Minion*
designed by Robert Slimbach and the display face *Lithos*
designed by Carol Twombly. Photography by
Rick Stafford of the Harvard University Art Museums

The expenses of publishing this volume
have been assumed by three friends of
The Houghton Library